Sustainable Success Blueprint

Building Businesses for Tomorrow

By

ALEX WALTER

Table of Contents

<u>Measuring and Reporting Impact</u>

<u>Conclusion</u>

Introduction

In an era defined by rapid technological advancements, shifting global landscapes, and heightened awareness of environmental and societal issues, the traditional notions of business success have undergone a profound transformation. No longer can prosperity be measured solely in financial terms; instead, a new paradigm has emerged, one that places equal emphasis on economic gains, ethical considerations, and the well-being of our planet and its inhabitants.

Welcome to "Sustainable Success Blueprint: Building Businesses for Tomorrow." Within the pages of this book, we embark on a journey that transcends the boundaries of conventional business wisdom. Here, we delve into a world where success is not just an outcome, but a deliberate and harmonious convergence of purpose, innovation, ethics, and collaboration.

In the pursuit of sustainable success, business leaders find themselves at a crossroads, where the choices they make today have far-reaching implications for the generations that follow. As the challenges of climate change, social inequality, and resource scarcity grow more urgent, the need for transformative action becomes undeniable. This book is designed to be your compass in this new landscape, guiding you toward building businesses that thrive not just for a fleeting moment, but for the long arc of time.

Through seven captivating chapters, we will explore the intricate web of concepts that underpin sustainable success. We will uncover the fundamental importance of purpose-driven businesses and ethical leadership, and we will learn how to leverage innovation as a tool for both growth and positive impact. Together, we will uncover the power of collaborative partnerships and ecosystems, and discover how the triple bottom line approach can redefine the parameters of prosperity.

Moreover, this book does not merely offer theoretical musings. It is a practical guide, brimming with real-world examples of businesses that have embraced sustainability as a driving force behind their strategies. From multinational corporations to innovative startups, each story serves as a testament to the fact that sustainable success is not an abstract dream, but a tangible reality within reach.

As you embark on this transformative journey through the chapters that follow, prepare to challenge your perceptions, expand your horizons, and equip yourself with the tools needed to lead businesses that are not just profitable, but purposeful. The time for change is now, and you hold the blueprint for building businesses that will shape a better tomorrow.

Chapter 1

Understanding Sustainable Success

Sustainable success refers to achieving long-term growth and prosperity while maintaining a balance between economic, environmental, and social factors. It involves making decisions that consider not only immediate gains, but also their impact on the planet and society over time. This approach often involves practices like responsible resource management, ethical business conduct, and a focus on innovation that benefits all stakeholders.

Imagine a successful business as a flourishing tree. For it to grow and thrive sustainably, its roots delve deep into three key soils: economics, environment, and society.

Economically, the tree's branches bear fruits of profit and growth. But rather than plucking all the fruit at once, sustainable success involves careful pruning and harvesting to ensure a consistent yield over the years. This allows the business to reinvest in its operations, nurture innovation, and weather economic storms.

Environmentally, the tree's roots intertwine with the soil, drawing nutrients and moisture. In the same way, sustainable success acknowledges that the environment provides resources essential for business. Just as a tree releases oxygen and supports other life, a sustainable business minimizes its ecological impact. It adopts eco-friendly practices, minimizes waste, and seeks renewable alternatives.

Socially, the tree stands tall in a community. Its branches provide shade and shelter to diverse life forms. In the realm of sustainable success, the business fosters relationships within society. It treats employees, customers, and communities with respect, promoting diversity, equality, and fair working conditions. It contributes positively to the world around it, enhancing social well-being.

The three soils – economics, environment, and society are intertwined. Neglecting one can weaken the entire structure. Just as a tree needs nurturing, care, and attention for it to stand the test of time, sustainable success requires a harmonious balance between profit, planet, and people. This synergy ensures that the tree of success not only survives, but thrives and flourishes for generations to come.

 Sustainable success in the context of modern business goes beyond short-term profit maximization and incorporates a comprehensive approach that considers economic, environmental, and social dimensions. Here's a detailed explanation:

1. Economic Dimension: At the core of sustainable success is the ability of a business to generate consistent and long-term economic value. This involves strategies that ensure steady revenue growth, efficient cost management, and strong financial performance.

However, the focus is not solely on immediate profits; instead, businesses strive to create value over time by fostering innovation, developing strong customer relationships, and adapting to changing market conditions.

2. Environmental Dimension: Businesses are increasingly recognizing the importance of minimizing their impact on the environment. Sustainable success involves adopting environmentally friendly practices that reduce carbon emissions, waste generation, and resource consumption.

This could include using renewable energy sources, optimizing supply chains to minimize transportation emissions, and implementing waste reduction strategies. By doing so, businesses contribute to a healthier planet and position themselves to thrive in an era of heightened environmental awareness.

3. Social Dimension: Businesses that achieve sustainable success prioritize social responsibility and positive societal impact. They engage in ethical business practices, treat their employees fairly, and actively contribute to the well-being of their communities. This could involve supporting local initiatives, promoting diversity and inclusion within the organization, and ensuring safe and ethical working conditions throughout the supply chain.

4. Innovation and Adaptability: In the rapidly changing landscape of modern business, sustainable success requires a commitment to continuous innovation and adaptability. Businesses that can identify emerging trends, technological advancements, and shifting customer preferences can proactively adjust their strategies to stay relevant and maintain their competitive edge.

5. Stakeholder Engagement: Successful businesses recognize that they are interconnected with a variety of stakeholders, including customers, employees, investors, suppliers, and the broader community. Engaging with these stakeholders in transparent and meaningful ways fosters trust, enhances reputation, and aligns business practices with the interests of all involved parties.

6. Long-Term Perspective: Sustainable success is driven by a long-term perspective rather than short-term gains. This involves making decisions that may not yield immediate benefits but contribute to the overall resilience and longevity of the business. For instance, investing in employee training, R&D, and sustainability initiatives may lead to slower returns

initially, but they set the stage for sustained growth and impact over time.

In essence, sustainable success in modern business is a holistic and integrated approach that seeks to create value for all stakeholders while ensuring the well-being of the planet. It requires a commitment to balancing economic prosperity, environmental stewardship, and social responsibility, driven by a long-term vision and a willingness to evolve in response to changing circumstances.

Importance of long-term thinking and responsible practices

Here are some key points highlighting the importance of long-term thinking and responsible practices:

1. Sustainability: Long-term thinking and responsible practices ensure the sustainability of resources and ecosystems. By considering the long run, we avoid depleting finite resources and damaging the environment, ensuring a better future for generations to come.

2. Ethical Considerations: Responsible practices take into account the ethical implications of actions. Long-term thinking helps prevent short-sighted decisions that might compromise ethical standards for immediate gains.

3. Economic Stability: Long-term planning fosters economic stability by promoting investments that yield returns over time. Responsible practices prevent reckless financial decisions that could lead to economic crises.

4. Innovation: A long-term perspective encourages innovation and research, leading to advancements in technology, medicine, and various fields. Responsible practices ensure that innovation doesn't come at the expense of safety or ethical concerns.

5. Corporate Reputation: Businesses practicing responsible behavior build a positive reputation, attracting customers, investors, and employees who value ethical conduct. Long-term thinking helps companies avoid scandals that can damage their reputation.

6. Social Progress: Responsible practices contribute to social progress by addressing societal challenges, such as poverty, inequality, and education. Long-term thinking supports sustainable development and positive social impact.

7. Resilience to Change: Long-term planning prepares individuals, organizations, and societies to adapt to unexpected changes and challenges. Responsible practices build resilience by considering potential risks and developing contingency plans.

8. Environmental Stewardship: Responsible practices protect the environment, conserving biodiversity and minimizing pollution. Long-term thinking ensures that ecosystems remain intact for future generations.

9. Health and Well-being: Long-term thinking in healthcare focuses on preventive measures, leading to healthier lifestyles and reduced healthcare costs. Responsible practices prioritize public health and safety.

10. Global Cooperation: Addressing complex global issues, such as climate change and pandemics, requires long-term thinking and responsible practices on an international scale. Cooperation among nations becomes crucial to achieve meaningful solutions.

11. Cultural Preservation: Long-term thinking values cultural heritage and traditions, aiming to preserve them for future generations. Responsible practices respect diverse cultures and histories.

12. Personal Fulfillment: Adopting responsible practices and a long-term perspective can lead to personal satisfaction, knowing that one's actions contribute positively to society and the environment.

In essence, the combination of long-term thinking and responsible practices ensures a balanced and sustainable approach to decision-making, benefiting individuals, communities, and the planet as a whole.

Chapter 2

The Foundation of Purpose-driven Business

The foundation of a purpose-driven business lies in its commitment to a clear and meaningful mission that goes beyond just financial profit. Such businesses prioritize creating positive social and environmental impact alongside their economic goals. They align their strategies, operations, and values with this broader purpose, aiming to contribute to the well-being of society and the planet.

This approach can enhance employee motivation, customer loyalty, and brand reputation, as people are increasingly drawn to companies that demonstrate genuine concern for societal issues. In essence, a purpose-driven business operates with the belief that profitability and positive impact are not mutually exclusive, but rather can reinforce each other for long-term sustainable success.

Let's delve deeper into the concept of a purpose-driven business:

1. Defining a Clear Purpose: At the core of a purpose-driven business is a well-defined and inspiring purpose that goes beyond mere profit generation. This purpose reflects the company's reason for existence, its values, and its contribution to society. It acts as a guiding star, providing direction for decision-making and strategy development.

2. Integration into Business Strategy: Purpose-driven businesses integrate their mission into every aspect of their operations, from product development to marketing, supply chain management, and employee engagement. This alignment ensures that the company's actions consistently reflect its purpose.

3. Long-Term Perspective: These businesses take a long-term view, understanding that societal and

environmental issues are interconnected with their success. By addressing these issues, they contribute to a sustainable and inclusive future, which can lead to greater resilience and relevance over time.

4. Stakeholder Engagement: Purpose-driven businesses recognize that they have a responsibility towards various stakeholders beyond just shareholders. This includes employees, customers, communities, suppliers, and the environment. They actively engage with these stakeholders to create positive relationships and mutual benefits.

5. Measurable Impact: Measurement and reporting of impact become crucial for purpose-driven businesses. They track and communicate the social and environmental outcomes of their actions, showing transparency and accountability to their stakeholders.

6. Employee Engagement and Attraction: A strong purpose resonates with employees and potential recruits who are seeking meaningful work. It can boost morale, foster a sense of belonging, and encourage innovation and collaboration.

7. Customer Loyalty: Consumers are increasingly drawn to brands that align with their own values and beliefs. Purpose-driven businesses can build strong brand loyalty by demonstrating a commitment to causes that matter to their customers.

8. Innovation and Adaptation: Pursuing a broader purpose often requires creativity and innovation to find new ways of doing business that align with the company's goals. This adaptability can lead to a competitive advantage in a rapidly changing world.

9. Global Challenges: Purpose-driven businesses often address pressing global challenges, such as poverty, climate change, inequality, and more. By taking proactive steps to address these challenges, they contribute to a better world while also strengthening their own reputation.

10. Part of a Broader Movement: The rise of purpose-driven businesses is part of a broader movement towards a more conscious and responsible approach to business. Governments, consumers, and investors are recognizing the importance of ethical and sustainable practices.

In summary, a purpose-driven business goes beyond profit as its primary motive and aligns its operations with a meaningful mission that addresses societal and environmental concerns. This approach not only contributes to a better world but also can lead to improved financial performance and enhanced reputation.

Role of purpose in driving sustainable success

The concept of purpose plays several key roles in driving sustainable success for businesses:

1. Guiding Decision-Making: A well-defined purpose provides a clear framework for making decisions at all levels of the organization. It helps steer choices that align with the company's long-term goals, values, and mission, ensuring consistency in actions and strategies.

2. Employee Motivation and Engagement: A strong purpose can inspire employees by giving them a sense of meaning and fulfillment in their work. When employees believe they are contributing to a larger purpose, their motivation, commitment, and

job satisfaction tend to increase, leading to higher productivity and retention rates.

3. Innovation and Adaptation: Purpose-driven businesses are more likely to be innovative and open to change. The pursuit of a meaningful mission encourages creative problem-solving, enabling companies to develop innovative products, services, and processes that address societal challenges.

4. Customer Loyalty and Brand Equity: Purpose resonates with consumers who prefer to support businesses that align with their values. Companies that actively pursue a positive social and environmental impact often build stronger customer loyalty, resulting in a more robust brand reputation and increased market share.

5. Long-Term Perspective: Purpose-driven businesses tend to adopt a long-term view, focusing on building a sustainable future rather than chasing short-term profits. This orientation can lead to more prudent financial decisions, reduced risk exposure, and enhanced resilience in the face of economic fluctuations.

6. Stakeholder Trust and Relationships: Purpose-driven businesses cultivate trust and positive relationships with various stakeholders, including employees, customers, suppliers, and communities. By demonstrating a commitment to social responsibility, these businesses foster goodwill and cooperation.

7. Talent Attraction and Retention: Purpose-driven companies are often attractive to top talent who seek meaningful work that goes beyond financial compensation. They can attract skilled individuals who want to contribute to a higher purpose, thereby strengthening the company's human capital.

8. Risk Mitigation: Companies that integrate purpose into their operations are more likely to anticipate and address emerging social and environmental risks. By proactively managing these risks, they can avoid potential controversies and reputational damage.

9. Responsible Resource Management: A focus on purpose encourages responsible management of resources, leading to reduced waste, energy consumption, and environmental impact. This can

lead to cost savings, operational efficiencies, and a reduced carbon footprint.

10. Positive Impact: Ultimately, the central role of purpose is to drive positive impact on society and the environment. By addressing critical issues, such as climate change, inequality, and poverty, purpose-driven businesses contribute to a more sustainable and equitable world.

However, purpose is not only a moral imperative but also a strategic asset that contributes to the long-term success of businesses. It guides decision-making, fosters innovation, enhances stakeholder relationships, and positions companies as agents of positive change in a rapidly evolving global landscape.

Case studies of businesses that have successfully aligned their purpose with profit

Here are a few case studies of businesses that have successfully aligned their purpose with profit:

1. Patagonia: The outdoor clothing and gear company Patagonia is known for its strong commitment to environmental sustainability. The company's mission is to "Build the best product, cause no unnecessary harm, and use business to inspire and implement solutions to the environmental crisis." Patagonia's dedication to environmental responsibility is reflected in its product materials, supply chain practices, and advocacy efforts. Despite its emphasis on sustainability, Patagonia has consistently grown its profits, showcasing how a purpose-driven approach can lead to both positive impact and financial success.

2. Unilever: Unilever is a global consumer goods company that has integrated social and environmental responsibility into its business model.

Through its Sustainable Living Plan, Unilever aims to improve the health and well-being of more than 1 billion people, reduce its environmental impact, and enhance the livelihoods of millions. This purpose-driven approach has not only aligned with its commitment to sustainability but has also contributed to revenue growth and brand loyalty among environmentally conscious consumers.

3. TOMS: TOMS is a footwear company with a unique "One for One" business model. For every pair of shoes purchased, TOMS donates a pair to a child in need. Additionally, TOMS expanded its model to include eyewear and coffee, each with a corresponding social impact initiative. This purpose-driven approach has resonated with consumers and helped the company achieve profitability while making a positive impact on communities around the world.

4. Danone: Danone, a multinational food-products corporation, has embraced a "dual project" approach, which aims to balance economic success with social progress. The company's mission is to bring health through food to as many people as possible. Danone's commitment to sustainability and

social responsibility has driven innovation in product development, packaging, and supply chain practices. This has resulted in improved financial performance, demonstrating that purpose-driven strategies can enhance profitability.

5. B Corps: B Corps are businesses that meet rigorous standards of social and environmental performance, accountability, and transparency. Many B Corps have successfully aligned their purpose with profit, such as Ben & Jerry's, which emphasizes social responsibility through fair trade practices and community engagement, while maintaining strong brand loyalty and growth.

These case studies illustrate that purpose-driven businesses can thrive while making positive contributions to society and the environment. They demonstrate that a clear and meaningful purpose can drive innovation, customer loyalty, employee engagement, and financial success, showcasing the potential for businesses to create value beyond profits.

Chapter 3

Ethical Leadership and Organizational Culture

Ethical leadership involves guiding an organization with a strong moral compass, making decisions that prioritize ethical principles and values. This kind of leadership sets the tone for the organizational culture, shaping the behaviors and values of employees.

A positive organizational culture, in turn, encourages ethical behavior, collaboration, and respect among team members. When leaders model ethical conduct and foster a culture of integrity, it can lead to better employee engagement, improved performance, and a stronger reputation for the organization.

Significance of ethical leadership in fostering a culture of sustainability

Ethical leadership plays a crucial role in fostering a culture of sustainability within an organization. By demonstrating ethical behavior, leaders set an example for employees to follow, which includes considering the long-term environmental, social, and economic impacts of their decisions and actions. Here's how ethical leadership contributes to a culture of sustainability:

1. Values Alignment: Ethical leaders prioritize sustainability values such as environmental stewardship, social responsibility, and economic viability. This encourages employees to align their actions with these values, creating a cohesive and purpose-driven culture.

2. Long-Term Perspective: Ethical leaders focus on the long-term consequences of decisions, ensuring that short-term gains do not compromise the well-being of future generations. This mindset encourages sustainable practices that preserve resources and minimize negative impacts.

3. Transparency and Accountability: Ethical leaders promote transparency in decision-making and hold themselves accountable for their actions. This transparency extends to sustainability efforts, encouraging open communication about environmental and social initiatives.

4. Stakeholder Engagement: Ethical leaders engage with stakeholders, including employees, customers, suppliers, and the community, to gather diverse perspectives and make informed decisions that benefit all parties involved. This inclusive approach often leads to more sustainable practices.

5. Innovation: Ethical leaders encourage innovation in finding sustainable solutions. They promote a culture where employees are empowered to come up with creative ideas for reducing waste, conserving resources, and improving efficiency.

6. Risk Management: Ethical leaders assess and mitigate risks associated with unsustainable practices, recognizing that ethical missteps can lead to reputational damage, legal issues, and financial setbacks.

7. Employee Engagement: A culture of sustainability driven by ethical leadership fosters a sense of purpose among employees. They are more likely to be engaged and committed when they feel their work contributes to positive environmental and social outcomes.

8. Learning and Development: Ethical leaders invest in educating employees about sustainability principles and best practices. This continuous learning empowers employees to make informed choices that align with the organization's sustainability goals.

9. Adaptability: Ethical leaders recognize that sustainability is an evolving concept. They encourage flexibility and adaptability to changing environmental and social circumstances, ensuring the organization remains resilient in the face of challenges.

10. Reputation and Brand Enhancement: Ethical leadership focused on sustainability can enhance an organization's reputation and brand. Consumers are increasingly drawn to businesses that demonstrate a commitment to ethical and sustainable practices,

leading to increased customer loyalty and market differentiation.

11. Attracting and Retaining Talent: Ethical leadership and a culture of sustainability attract employees who share similar values. Younger generations, in particular, prioritize working for organizations that contribute positively to society and the environment. This can help with talent recruitment and retention.

12. Regulatory Compliance: Ethical leaders ensure that the organization complies with relevant environmental and social regulations. By adhering to these standards, the organization avoids legal troubles and potential fines, while also minimizing negative impacts on the environment and society.

13. Collaboration and Partnerships: Ethical leadership encourages collaboration with other organizations, NGOs, government bodies, and community groups. Such partnerships can amplify the organization's sustainability efforts and drive systemic change.

14. Resilience and Adaptation: A culture of sustainability fosters adaptability, enabling the organization to respond effectively to changing market conditions and emerging sustainability challenges. Ethical leaders guide the organization in making necessary adjustments to remain competitive and relevant.

15. Reduction of Waste and Costs: Ethical leaders promote resource efficiency and waste reduction initiatives, which can lead to cost savings. By minimizing waste and optimizing resource use, the organization becomes more efficient and financially sustainable.

16. Global Impact: Organizations with ethical leaders who champion sustainability contribute to global efforts to address pressing environmental and social issues, such as climate change, poverty, and inequality. This broader impact helps create a better world for everyone.

17. Influence on Industry Norms: Ethical leaders can influence industry norms and practices. When organizations take a proactive stance on sustainability, they set a standard that encourages

others within the industry to follow suit, driving positive change on a larger scale.

18. Ethical Supply Chain: Ethical leaders extend their commitment to sustainability beyond the organization itself and into its supply chain. This ensures that suppliers and partners also adhere to ethical and sustainable practices, creating a more holistic impact.

19. Risk Mitigation: Ethical leadership addresses potential risks associated with unsustainable practices, such as supply chain disruptions due to resource scarcity or reputational damage from negative social or environmental impacts.

20. Interconnectedness of Issues: Ethical leaders recognize the interconnectedness of social, environmental, and economic issues. By promoting a holistic approach to decision-making, they ensure that sustainability initiatives consider multiple facets of well-being.

Ethical leadership is a driving force that shapes an organization's commitment to sustainability, influencing behavior, decision-making, and culture.

Its significance extends to various aspects of the organization's operations, impact, and relationships, ultimately contributing to a more sustainable and responsible business model.

Overall, ethical leadership serves as the guiding force that shapes an organization's commitment to sustainability. When leaders demonstrate integrity, empathy, and a strong sense of responsibility, they inspire employees to contribute to a culture that prioritizes the well-being of people, the planet, and future generations.

Strategies for creating an ethical and values-driven organizational culture

Creating an ethical and values-driven organizational culture involves several key strategies:

1. Clear Values Definition: Clearly define the organization's core values and ensure they align with its mission and goals.

2. Leadership Role Modeling: Leaders should embody the values and ethical behavior they expect from employees, setting a positive example.

3. Communication: Regularly communicate the importance of ethical behavior and values through various channels, such as meetings, emails, and training sessions.

4. Code of Conduct: Develop a comprehensive code of conduct that outlines expected behavior and consequences for unethical actions.

5. Training and Education: Provide ongoing training to employees about ethics, values, and decision-making to ensure they understand and apply these principles.

6. Incentives and Recognition: Reward employees who consistently demonstrate ethical behavior and align with the organization's values.

7. Transparent Decision-Making: Make decisions transparently, involving relevant stakeholders when appropriate, to build trust and ensure fairness.

8. Whistleblower Protection: Establish a safe and confidential mechanism for employees to report ethical concerns without fear of retaliation.

9. Diverse and Inclusive Environment: Foster a diverse and inclusive workplace, where different perspectives can contribute to ethical discussions.

10. Ethics Committees: Form committees or boards to oversee ethical matters, ensuring accountability and consistency.

11. Regular Assessments: Periodically evaluate the organization's ethical culture to identify areas for improvement and address emerging issues.

12. Customer and Stakeholder Engagement: Engage with customers, clients, and stakeholders to understand their expectations and concerns, and integrate their feedback into decision-making.

13. Sustainability Practices: Integrate environmentally and socially responsible practices into business operations, aligning with ethical values.

14. Consequences for Violations: Consistently enforce consequences for ethical violations, demonstrating the organization's commitment to its values.

15. Adaptability: Continuously adapt the ethical culture to changing circumstances and challenges, ensuring it remains relevant and effective.

Remember that building an ethical and values-driven culture is an ongoing process that requires commitment, consistency, and effort from all levels of the organization.

Chapter 4

Innovation for a Changing World

Innovation for a Changing World reflects the importance of adapting and creating new solutions in response to evolving challenges and opportunities. It highlights the need for creative thinking, technological advancements, and sustainable practices to address the dynamic nature of our global society.

Role of innovation in adapting to environmental and societal change

Innovation plays a crucial role in adapting to environmental and societal changes by enabling the development of new solutions, technologies, and approaches. It helps address challenges such as climate change, resource scarcity, and social inequality. By fostering creativity and collaboration, innovation allows us to:

1. Environmental Sustainability: Innovation leads to the creation of cleaner energy sources, efficient waste management systems, and sustainable agriculture practices. It drives the development of technologies like renewable energy, electric vehicles, and green building materials.

2. Resilience: Innovations help communities prepare for and respond to natural disasters and other environmental shocks. This includes early warning systems, disaster-resistant infrastructure, and adaptive farming techniques.

3. Social Equality: Innovation can address societal issues like poverty, access to education, and healthcare. Through digital solutions, remote learning platforms, and telemedicine, innovation bridges gaps and makes essential services more accessible.

4. Circular Economy: Innovations in recycling, upcycling, and waste reduction contribute to a circular economy, where resources are used efficiently and waste is minimized.

5. Digital Transformation: Technological innovations drive digital transformation, enhancing communication, connectivity, and access to information, especially in remote or underserved areas.

6. Collaboration: Innovation often requires cross-sector collaboration, bringing together governments, businesses, academia, and nonprofits to collectively tackle complex challenges.

7. Adaptive Solutions: Innovations provide adaptable solutions that can evolve with changing circumstances, ensuring their effectiveness over time.

8. Policy Support: Innovative ideas can influence policy changes, encouraging governments to implement regulations that promote sustainability and equality.

9. Behavioral Change: Innovation can shape behavior by creating user-friendly tools that encourage sustainable practices, such as energy-efficient appliances or apps that promote eco-friendly lifestyles.

10. Learning from Nature: Biomimicry, an innovative approach, draws inspiration from nature's solutions to create sustainable designs and technologies.

In essence, innovation empowers societies to respond to dynamic environmental and societal shifts, fostering resilience, sustainability, and progress.

How innovation can lead to competitive advantage while addressing global challenges

Innovation can indeed lead to competitive advantage while addressing global challenges by allowing businesses to differentiate themselves, create value, and adapt to changing circumstances. Here's how:

1. Market Differentiation: Businesses that innovate to address global challenges often create unique products, services, or approaches that stand out in the market. This differentiation can attract

environmentally and socially conscious consumers who prioritize sustainable and responsible options.

2. Early Mover Advantage: Being an early adopter of innovative solutions positions a company as a leader in addressing global challenges. This can help build brand loyalty and capture a larger market share before competitors catch up.

3. Cost Efficiency: Innovations that improve efficiency, reduce waste, or streamline processes can lead to cost savings. Sustainable practices, for example, can lower operational costs through reduced resource consumption.

4. Access to New Markets: Innovations that cater to global challenges can open doors to new markets where demand for sustainable and responsible solutions is growing.

5. Long-Term Viability: Businesses that proactively address global challenges through innovation are better equipped to withstand regulatory changes and evolving consumer preferences. This enhances their long-term viability.

6. Reputation and Brand Enhancement: Companies that champion innovative solutions for global challenges enhance their brand reputation, portraying themselves as responsible and socially conscious entities. This can lead to increased customer loyalty and positive word-of-mouth.

7. Talent Attraction and Retention: Companies committed to addressing global challenges through innovation often attract top talent seeking purpose-driven work environments. Employees are more likely to stay with companies that align with their values.

8. Partnerships and Collaborations: Innovative initiatives addressing global challenges can attract collaborations with governments, NGOs, academia, and other businesses. These partnerships can amplify impact and enhance a company's influence.

9. Adaptation to Change: Businesses that innovate are better equipped to adapt to unforeseen changes, including shifts in regulations, resource availability, or market demands.

10. Sustainable Growth: Innovation that focuses on sustainability and global challenges ensures growth that is aligned with the well-being of people and the planet, leading to more stable and resilient long-term growth.

11. Learning and Improvement: The process of innovating to address global challenges encourages continuous learning, improvement, and a culture of adaptability within a company.

By strategically integrating innovation into their operations, businesses can not only address critical global challenges but also gain a competitive edge, ensuring their relevance and success in an ever-changing world.

Chapter 5

The Triple Bottom Line Approach

The Triple Bottom Line (TBL) approach is a framework that evaluates an organization's performance and impact based on three dimensions: social, environmental, and financial. It goes beyond traditional financial metrics to include social and environmental considerations. Here's a breakdown of each dimension:

1. Social Dimension: This aspect focuses on the social impact and contributions of an organization. It involves considerations such as employee well-being, community engagement, human rights, labor practices, diversity and inclusion, and the overall positive influence a company has on society.

2. Environmental Dimension: This dimension assesses an organization's ecological impact and

efforts to promote sustainability. It involves factors like resource conservation, waste reduction, carbon footprint, pollution control, and the adoption of environmentally friendly practices.

3. Financial Dimension: This is the traditional economic aspect that evaluates a company's financial performance, profitability, and economic growth. It includes metrics like revenue, profit margins, return on investment (ROI), and shareholder value.

The Triple Bottom Line approach encourages businesses to adopt a holistic perspective, considering their impact on people, planet, and profits. Rather than focusing solely on short-term financial gains, organizations are encouraged to make decisions that align with sustainable development, long-term viability, and positive societal outcomes.

Benefits of the Triple Bottom Line approach include

- Long-Term Sustainability: By addressing social and environmental aspects, companies ensure their operations are sustainable and aligned with global challenges.

- Stakeholder Engagement: Organizations engage stakeholders beyond shareholders, including employees, customers, communities, and regulators.

- Innovation: A focus on social and environmental concerns often drives innovative solutions, leading to competitive advantages.

- Risk Management: Addressing environmental and social issues can mitigate risks associated with regulatory changes and reputational damage.

- Resilience: Businesses that consider all three dimensions are better equipped to adapt to changing market conditions and societal expectations.

The Triple Bottom Line approach encourages a more responsible and balanced way of doing business, contributing to a world where economic prosperity, social equity, and environmental stewardship are integrated goals.

Introducing the concept of the triple bottom line: People, Planet, Profit

The concept of the Triple Bottom Line (TBL) revolves around three interconnected pillars: People, Planet, and Profit. It is a holistic framework that encourages organizations to evaluate their performance and impact through a multidimensional lens, extending beyond mere financial considerations. The three pillars represent:

1. People: This dimension focuses on the social impact and well-being of stakeholders within and outside the organization. It encompasses fair labor practices, employee health and safety, community engagement, diversity and inclusion, and overall contributions to societal welfare.

2. Planet: The environmental dimension emphasizes an organization's ecological footprint and efforts toward sustainability. It involves responsible resource management, pollution reduction, carbon neutrality, conservation initiatives, and the adoption of environmentally friendly practices.

3. Profit: While the traditional economic bottom line remains important, the TBL approach expands the understanding of profitability. It encourages businesses to consider financial gains in harmony with social and environmental responsibilities. Financial success is not viewed as an isolated goal but as a means to support positive outcomes for people and the planet.

By embracing the Triple Bottom Line approach, organizations aim to create a balance among these three pillars, striving for shared value creation. This means pursuing strategies and initiatives that contribute positively to society, minimize environmental harm, and ensure economic prosperity. The TBL concept underscores the interdependence of these pillars and the necessity of addressing global challenges through a holistic and sustainable perspective.

How businesses can balance social, environmental, and financial goals

Businesses can effectively balance social, environmental, and financial goals by integrating strategies and practices that align with the Triple Bottom Line (TBL) approach. Here's how they can do it:

Social Goals

1.Employee Well-being: Prioritize fair wages, safe working conditions, and opportunities for professional growth. Offer wellness programs to support physical and mental health.

2. Diversity and Inclusion: Promote a diverse workforce and create an inclusive environment that values different perspectives and backgrounds.

3. Community Engagement: Participate in community initiatives, support local causes, and engage in philanthropic activities that positively

impact the communities in which the business operates.

Environmental Goals

1.Sustainable Practices: Adopt eco-friendly processes, such as reducing waste, conserving resources, and minimizing energy consumption.

2. Product Sustainability: Design products with a reduced environmental footprint and consider their entire lifecycle, from production to disposal.

3. Renewable Energy: Transition to renewable energy sources to reduce carbon emissions and environmental impact.

4. Supply Chain Responsibility: Collaborate with suppliers who adhere to sustainable practices, reducing the overall environmental footprint of the supply chain.

Financial Goals

1.Efficiency Improvements: Implement cost-saving measures through process optimization, waste reduction, and energy efficiency.

2. Long-Term Value: Invest in sustainable technologies, which may have higher upfront costs but lead to long-term savings and reduced operational risks.

3. Innovative Solutions: Develop products and services that address societal and environmental needs, tapping into emerging market demands.

4. Transparency and Reporting: Provide clear financial and non-financial reporting, showcasing the organization's commitment to the TBL approach.

Strategies that consider the interconnectedness of the three pillars

Strategic Alignment: Ensure that business strategies are aligned with all three dimensions, and incorporate social and environmental considerations into decision-making processes.

Cross-Functional Collaboration: Encourage collaboration among different departments to implement TBL initiatives and share insights.

Stakeholder Engagement: Listen to and involve stakeholders to better understand their needs, concerns, and expectations related to the TBL approach.

Measurement and Metrics: Develop key performance indicators (KPIs) to track progress in each dimension and hold the organization accountable for its TBL goals.

Ultimately, achieving a balanced Triple Bottom Line requires a commitment to sustainability, responsible business practices, and a willingness to adapt and innovate in order to create lasting positive impacts on society, the environment, and financial performance.

Chapter 6

Collaborative Partnerships and Ecosystems

Collaborative partnerships and ecosystems involve the cooperation and interaction of various organizations, stakeholders, and entities to achieve common goals. This approach recognizes that addressing complex challenges often requires a collective effort, pooling resources, expertise, and perspectives. Here's how collaborative partnerships and ecosystems work:

Partnership Types

- Business-Business Collaborations: Companies from different industries join forces to combine their strengths and resources, creating innovative solutions and reaching new markets.

- Business-Nonprofit Collaborations: Businesses partner with nonprofit organizations to address social and environmental issues, leveraging their respective expertise and resources.

- Public-Private Partnerships: Governments and private sector entities collaborate to tackle societal challenges, such as infrastructure development, healthcare, and education.

- Academia-Industry Collaborations: Educational institutions and businesses collaborate on research, development, and innovation to create new technologies and solutions.

Benefits

- Shared Expertise: Collaborators bring diverse skills and knowledge to the table, leading to better problem-solving and innovation.

- Resource Sharing: Partners pool resources, reducing costs and maximizing efficiency in addressing challenges.

- Access to New Markets: Collaboration can lead to market expansion by tapping into each partner's customer base.

- Risk Sharing: Partnerships can help mitigate risks associated with innovation and market entry by sharing the burden.

- Enhanced Impact: Collaborative efforts can have a broader and more profound impact than individual actions.

Ecosystem Approach

- Network of Relationships: An ecosystem includes various entities, including businesses, startups, investors, governments, and research institutions, all interconnected to create value.

- Innovation Hubs: Ecosystems often cluster around innovation hubs, such as technology parks or innovation districts, fostering idea exchange and collaboration.

- Supportive Environment: Ecosystems offer a nurturing environment for startups and entrepreneurs, providing access to resources, mentorship, and funding.

Challenges

-Alignment: Different partners may have varying goals and priorities that need to be aligned for effective collaboration.

- Communication: Effective communication and clear expectations are essential to avoid misunderstandings and conflicts.

- Intellectual Property: Partners need to address intellectual property rights and ownership of jointly developed solutions.

- Cultural Differences: Diverse partners may have different working cultures, requiring understanding and adaptation.

Collaborative partnerships and ecosystems are integral to addressing complex global challenges and achieving sustainable development. They foster collective creativity, innovation, and the leverage of combined resources, ultimately leading to more impactful and holistic solutions.

The power of collaboration with stakeholders, competitors, and governments

Collaboration with stakeholders, competitors, and governments can yield significant benefits, such as fostering innovation, addressing complex challenges, and creating a more favorable business environment. It can lead to shared resources, knowledge exchange, and improved solutions that might not have been possible individually. However, it's important to navigate potential conflicts of interest and maintain transparency to ensure successful collaboration.

Here are a few examples of businesses that have thrived through ecosystem-based thinking:

1. Apple's App Store: Apple created an ecosystem where developers could create and sell apps through the App Store. This not only generated revenue for Apple but also provided developers with a platform

to reach a massive user base. The collaboration between Apple and app developers resulted in a thriving app ecosystem.

2. Tesla's Supercharger Network: Tesla strategically built a network of superchargers for its electric vehicles. This ecosystem not only made Tesla's cars more appealing by addressing charging infrastructure concerns but also encouraged the adoption of electric vehicles as a whole. Tesla's investment in charging technology benefited the entire electric vehicle industry.

3. Alibaba Group: Alibaba's ecosystem includes e-commerce, cloud computing, digital payments, and more. Through platforms like Alibaba.com, Taobao, and Alipay, the company has created a comprehensive ecosystem that empowers businesses to reach customers, access financial services, and utilize cloud resources, all within the same ecosystem.

4. Starbucks Rewards Program: Starbucks built an ecosystem around its rewards program, offering customers loyalty points, discounts, and personalized recommendations. This program not

only increased customer engagement and loyalty but also provided valuable data to Starbucks, enabling them to tailor their offerings based on customer preferences.

5. Airbnb: Airbnb's ecosystem connects hosts with travelers seeking accommodations. By creating a platform that leverages underutilized spaces, Airbnb not only offers unique travel experiences but also allows hosts to monetize their properties. This collaborative approach disrupted the traditional hospitality industry.

6. Open Source Software Communities: Businesses like Red Hat have thrived by contributing to and leveraging open source software ecosystems. By collaborating with developers globally, these companies build valuable products and services while benefiting from the collective expertise of the open source community.

In these examples, businesses have harnessed the power of collaboration, strategic partnerships, and shared resources to create thriving ecosystems that benefit multiple stakeholders, including customers, partners, and even competitors.

Chapter 7

Measuring and Reporting Impact

Measuring sustainability performance involves using various metrics and tools to assess environmental, social, and economic impacts. Common metrics include carbon footprint, water usage, waste generation, and social indicators like employee well-being. Tools such as Life Cycle Assessment (LCA), Environmental Impact Assessment (EIA), and Global Reporting Initiative (GRI) reporting can help organizations evaluate and communicate their sustainability efforts. The choice of metrics and tools depends on the specific context and goals of the assessment.

The importance of transparently reporting impact to stakeholders

Transparently reporting sustainability impact to stakeholders is crucial for several reasons:

1. Accountability: Transparent reporting holds organizations accountable for their sustainability goals and actions. It demonstrates a commitment to addressing environmental and social issues, fostering trust among stakeholders.

2. Credibility: Openly sharing data and progress showcases an organization's credibility. It allows stakeholders to verify claims and evaluate the effectiveness of sustainability initiatives.

3. Engagement: Transparent reporting engages stakeholders by involving them in the journey towards sustainability. It encourages collaboration, feedback, and shared responsibility in achieving sustainable outcomes.

4. Decision-making: Clear reporting provides stakeholders with valuable information for making informed decisions. Investors, customers, and

employees can better assess the organization's values and align their choices accordingly.

5. Risk Management: Identifying and addressing sustainability risks becomes more effective when stakeholders are well-informed. Transparent reporting helps organizations mitigate potential negative impacts.

6. Innovation: Sharing successes and challenges can inspire innovation. Stakeholder feedback can lead to new ideas and approaches that enhance sustainability performance.

7. Regulatory Compliance: Transparent reporting ensures adherence to regulations and standards, which is important for avoiding legal and reputational risks.

8. Market Competitiveness: Organizations that transparently report their sustainability efforts often gain a competitive edge. Increasingly, consumers and investors prefer businesses with a strong commitment to sustainable practices.

9. Long-Term Strategy: Transparent reporting provides a platform for communicating long-term sustainability strategies, demonstrating that sustainability is an integral part of the organization's vision.

10. Transparency as a Value: By embracing transparent reporting, organizations communicate that transparency itself is a core value, fostering a culture of openness and accountability.

In summary, transparent reporting of sustainability impact strengthens an organization's reputation, enhances stakeholder relationships, and contributes to positive environmental and social change.

Conclusion

In the pursuit of a more sustainable future, "Sustainable Success Blueprint: Building Businesses for Tomorrow" serves as a guiding light, illuminating the path toward responsible and impactful entrepreneurship. This blueprint reminds us that success is not merely defined by short-term gains, but by the enduring legacy we leave for generations to come.

As we navigate the intricate interplay between economic prosperity, environmental stewardship, and social equity, this blueprint empowers us to construct businesses that stand not just for profit, but for purpose. By weaving sustainability into the very fabric of our strategies, we ensure that our ventures not only thrive today, but also serve as beacons of inspiration and innovation, lighting the way for a harmonious coexistence of business and the planet.

So let this blueprint be our compass, guiding us as we build enterprises that not only weather the challenges of today, but also lay the foundation for a world where both prosperity and sustainability flourish hand in hand. The journey towards a sustainable future requires a deliberate and collective effort. As we close this transformative guide, we're reminded that sustainability isn't an isolated endeavor; it's a symphony of interconnected actions, woven together by the threads of responsibility, innovation, and conscious decision-making.

This blueprint doesn't just mark an end; it marks a new beginning—a call to action that echoes beyond the pages. It's a rallying cry for leaders, entrepreneurs, and change-makers to unite under a common purpose: the betterment of our planet and society. Through the stories shared, the strategies outlined, and the wisdom imparted, we're equipped with the tools to forge a path that redefines success in the context of our shared world.

In the grand tapestry of time, the success stories we create won't be measured solely by financial gains or market dominance. They'll be measured by the positive ripples we set in motion—the cleaner air, the empowered communities, the restored ecosystems. This blueprint is more than a manual;

it's an invitation to participate in a movement that transcends boundaries and timelines.

As we turn the last page, let's remember that the blueprint's true power lies in its application. Let's be the architects of change, weaving these lessons into the very fabric of our businesses and weaving our businesses into the tapestry of sustainability. Let's build not just for today, but for tomorrow—for a world where the notion of success harmonizes with the ideals of enduring prosperity, leaving a legacy that echoes through the ages.